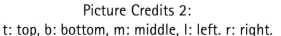

Copyright © 2013 North Parade Publishing Ltd.
4-5 North Parade, Bath, England. BA1 1LF
www.nppbooks.co.uk

American Edition Editor
Sean Kennelly

First Published: 2007

Caring for Dogs and Puppies

CONTENTS

Understanding Your Dog or Puppy

Buying a dog or puppy is a huge responsibility. You must ensure that your new pet is comfortable and healthy and you must care for it too.

A dog relies heavily on its sense of smell. Allow it to sniff you often so that it learns to recognize you

First Things First

At first, you and your surroundings will be new to your dog or puppy. It is important to communicate with it in a loving manner right from the beginning so that it can learn to trust you and form a bond with you.

Settling Down

Any dog or puppy will be restless in its new surroundings and it is your responsibility to make it feel wanted and cared for. Do not try to teach it to do tricks on the first day, nor force it to do things it does not want to do. Introduce it to your house and all the family members so that it feels like a part of your family.

To Show You Care

Bringing a dog or puppy home is a big responsibility. You have to look after your pet like you would look after a baby. Your dog or puppy's health depends entirely on you. With the support of your family, you have to look after the diet of your pet. You also have to take the time to walk your dog or puppy regularly so that it gets its exercise. You will need to teach it manners so that it does not upset other family members or mess up the house.

Top Tips

You should let your dog or puppy smell everything around the house when it arrives for the first time. This will introduce your dog or puppy to the house and make it feel at home.

With a little love and affection your dog will become a part of your happy family!

Exercise is as important for your dog or puppy as it is for you

7

One and Many

When buying a dog or puppy, it is important for you to know the different breeds available and the one that is most suitable to you and your family.

Breeds and All

There are two types of dogs — purebred and mixed breed. Each breed of dog has a distinct personality. Other factors that you must also keep in mind are the temperament, size of the dog, and its coat. Some breeds have traits, like hyperactivity or a tendency for barking, that may be a problem for you.

🐾 The fox terrier got its name as it was traditionally used to help hunt foxes

🐾 A dog is supposed to be a very loyal animal. Your dog can be your best friend

Little Fox

The fox terrier refers to two different breeds of dog: the smooth fox terrier and the wire fox terrier. The two terrier breeds are distinguished by their coats. The smooth fox terrier has a smooth, flat and dense coat, while the wire fox terrier has a coat with a dense, wiry texture. Both these breeds of terrier are quite friendly and enjoy being a part of the family and so make good pets.

Gentle Giants

The St. Bernard dog is a large breed of dog. There are two varieties of the breed — the smooth-coat and the rough-coat variety. The St. Bernard is an excellent choice as a family dog. They also make good watchdogs. Their sheer size can scare strangers! However, they are actually quite gentle. St. Bernards grow and gain weight very quickly. They can be prone to weak bones if they do not get proper food and exercise.

The St. Bernard is the heaviest breed of dog in the world!

Because of their good looks poodles are frequently seen in dog shows

Common Questions

Which is the most famous St. Bernard?

Barry, the brave St. Bernard, saved many lives. There is a monument to Barry in the famous Cimetière des Chiens (cemetery of dogs) near Paris, France, and his body is preserved in the Natural History Museum in Berne, Switzerland.

Dainty Poodle

Poodles comes in three sizes — standard, miniature and toy. The hair on the animal's body is curly and forms small clumps of curly ringlets. Poodles are intelligent, alert, and active. They are excellent watchdogs and are good pets. Poodles are also very easy to train.

The One I Want

After you have chosen the breed of dog or puppy you want to buy, there are some other things that you have to keep in mind before making the final decision.

How Do I Buy?

Try to buy your dog or puppy directly from a breeder. They will be able to tell you about the nature of each dog or puppy under their care. See for yourself how the puppy or the dog reacts when you try to pet it. If it is friendly at first, it is more likely to stay friendly when you take it home. You also have to decide whether you want a male or a female dog.

Common Questions

**Where else could I buy
my dog or puppy from?**

You could buy your dog or puppy
from a rescue organization.
These organizations find homes
for dogs and puppies that have
been abandoned and have no home.
These organizations also rescue
dogs and puppies when they are
not being treated properly.

Going To a Pet Shop

You can buy your dog or puppy from a
pet shop. While this is common, you
should consider some things carefully
before you do. A pet shop is unlikely to
have as much knowledge of a
particular dog or puppy that a breeder
would have. Ask about the background
of the dog or puppy and what its vet
history is in terms of vaccinations.

*Dogs in animal shelters and rescue
organizations wait eagerly for a good home.
You could take one as your pet and care for it*

Animal Shelters

An animal shelter is a good option if you
want to give an orphaned dog or puppy a
new home. Many dogs and puppies there will
have been with a family before, so they
might already be housetrained. Be aware
though: sadly, some will have been
mistreated in the past. You will have to love
them to earn their confidence and trust.

Giving It a Home

Once you buy your dog or puppy, the next big step is to take it home with you and teach it to adjust to its new surroundings.

It is usually easier for puppies to adapt to new surroundings than dogs. But remember, puppies need more attention than dogs

Comfort

Removing your dog or puppy from its familiar surroundings and making it settle down in your home can be quite a challenge. Get a new dog basket which it can call its own. It is also a good idea to initially use a blanket or a towel that it used in its previous home, as this will give it a sense of security. For the first few days or weeks, try not to leave your dog or puppy completely alone at home for too long. Being alone may scare it and make it irritable.

A Place to Stay

Just as you have your own room, your dog or puppy should have its own too! Find a warm and quiet place for the dog basket and then try not to move it too much so that your pet becomes comfortable. It is best to not allow your dog or puppy to sleep on the floor, sofa, couch or your bed as this encourages bad habits. Line your dog basket with a blanket to make it cozy and comfortable. When your dog or puppy is sleeping try not to disturb it.

Top Tips

Select a place for your dog or puppy's food and water bowls that is easily accessible to them, but out of the way of human feet. Once selected, keep the bowls in the same place. This way your dog or puppy will learn good food habits and won't be confused.

A Home of its Own

Your dog or puppy will want to make its basket its own space, so don't let any other pets go in the basket. The dog basket should be kept in the room where everyone in the family spends a lot of time. This will help it feel loved and a part of the family.

In some countries, larger dogs are kept outdoors in kennels

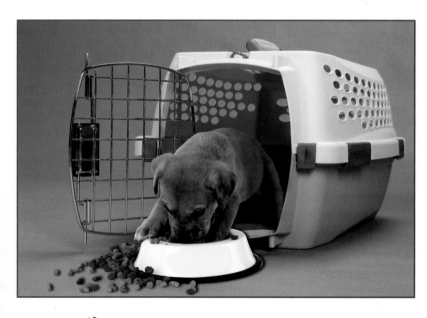

Many dogs and puppies feel at home in their own crate.

Making Friends

Once you've brought your dog or puppy home, you need to make it your companion and best friend.

You must make your dog or puppy feel comfortable in your home. This will help it become a faithful companion

A New Friend

To make sure that having a new dog or puppy at home is a happy experience, you should pay attention to the new pet's care and training closely. If you are friendly with your dog or puppy it will respond in a simlar way. Training your dog or puppy to listen to you or learn tricks can take some time. You have to be patient and keep trying until it learns.

Strict Rules

Make sure you do not get hurt when you play with your pet. Always use a toy during play, and throw the toy around so that your dog or puppy can run and fetch it. You must not play rough games with your dog or puppy because it might be cruel and your pet may be encouraged to bite. Buy toys your pet can chew on to discourage it from chewing things in the house that it shouldn't!

Dogs and puppies enjoy chewing bones as these make their teeth stronger

Water bowl

Things around the House

There are various things you can keep in the house to make your dog or puppy feel comfortable.

Food bowl

Dog collar

Common Questions

What should I do if my dog or puppy gets lost?

Do not panic if you cannot find your dog or puppy. Pets often run out of the house but come back soon. However, if your pet is missing, you could put an advertisement in the newspaper with a photograph of your pet. You could also contact animal shelters and rescue groups in your area.

Chewy dog bone

Dry dog food

Dog cage

Feeding Habits

The health of your dog or puppy depends on you. You should give it a proper and balanced diet to keep it healthy and strong.

Ground Rules

Your dog or puppy should be fed twice a day. You should have fixed hours to feed your pet. Serve the food in a clean dish and put the dish in a place where your pet will not be distracted by something else while eating. If you have more than one pet, then feed each of them separately. This way you will know how much food each pet needs. This will also prevent one pet from eating up the food of another.

Your dog or puppy should have a clean bowl of its own to eat from

You should never over-feed your dog or puppy as this might lead to obesity and other health problems

Balanced Diet

Just like your diet, your pet's diet should have a proper balance of carbohydrates, fats, proteins, vitamins and minerals. Packaged dog food usually contains a proper mix. But remember that the appetite of dogs or puppies varies from breed to breed. Your pet should have clean drinking water throughout the day. But do not allow your dog or puppy to drink water just before a meal as this will spoil its appetite.

Dog biscuits are available in various shapes and tastes and make good treats for your pet dog or puppy

You must make sure that the dog food you feed your dog or puppy has all the ingredients necessary for its growth

Top Tips

Ask the vet if your pet needs any special vitamin or mineral supplements.

Some dog breeds need supplements to maintain a healthy coat and skin and good bone growth.

Delicious Food

Meat is an important part of the diet for dogs and puppies. You can buy meat in tins for your dog or puppy, but alternate this wet food with dry food for a balanced diet. You can also give your dog or puppy the odd scrap of leftover cooked meat as a treat, but don't give them too much as they are not designed to eat cooked meat.

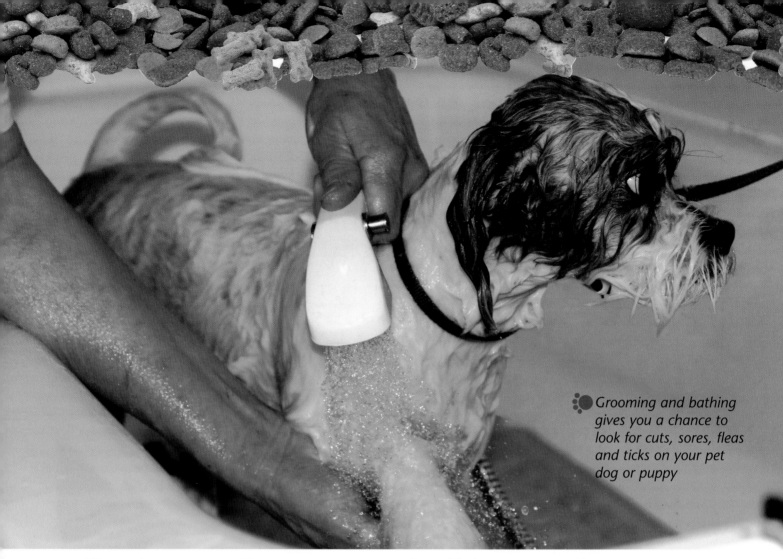

Grooming and bathing gives you a chance to look for cuts, sores, fleas and ticks on your pet dog or puppy

Grooming and Cleaning

Once you have a dog or puppy at home, it is essential to keep it clean and well groomed.

Groomed and Dressed

All dogs and puppies need to be groomed, but the frequency varies between breeds. Some dogs and puppies may need more frequent grooming than others. The most essential part of grooming is brushing and combing the hair of your pet, which helps to keep their coat shiny and skin healthy and free from ticks. A dog or puppy that has a long-haired coat should be brushed more frequently than one with short hair.

Washed and Cleaned

Dogs and puppies do not need to be bathed frequently. In fact, frequent bathing makes the skin of your pet dry as the natural oils present in the skin are lost. This can lead to infection and itching. While giving your pet a bath, use a good shampoo and conditioner designed for the coat of your pet. Make sure that you gently wipe your pet with a soft towel after you give it a bath.

Dog cologne

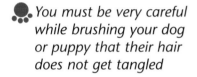 *You must be very careful while brushing your dog or puppy that their hair does not get tangled*

Dog hair-brush

Fine-toothed comb

Grooming Tools

Here are some basic grooming tools for your pet:
- Fine Tooth Comb
- Grooming Brush
- Shedding Blades
- Small Scissors
- Tweezers
- Soft Wipes
- Dog Cologne
- Dog Mat
- Nail Clipper

Dog mat

Dog-nail clipper

Common Questions

Do I need to find a professional groomer for my pet?

You may need a professional groomer if you do not have the time to clean and groom your pet. There are some breeds, like the poodle, that should have their coats styled in a particular way. It may be a good idea to take these dogs or puppies to a professional groomer once every couple of months.

Ticking Away

You must always ensure that your pet is free of ticks and fleas. They are not only harmful for your pet, but for you as well.

🐾 *A tick may be a tiny insect but it can be very dangerous. It will suck your pet's blood, which causes sores. Left untreated these sores may cause infection*

Flea Attack

Fleas are the most common pests of dogs and puppies. If you find your pet scratching itself continuously, or if it has developed a skin rash, it has probably been attacked by fleas. When fleas bite a dog or puppy, it may develop red bumps on its tail and on the sides of its hind legs. You can use anti-flea shampoos and soaps for mild infections. But if it is a serious attack, you have to take your pet to the vet for proper medication.

!

Top Tips

Always make sure that you use a fine-toothed comb to clean fleas off your dog or puppy. The fleas get caught between the fine teeth easily. After that, drop the comb into a bowl of soapy water. This will kill the fleas at once.

A dog or puppy can pick up fleas from other dogs when taken out for walks, so it is a good idea to groom it afterwards

Ticking Pests

After fleas, ticks are the most common pests picked up by dogs and puppies. Look for them especially in the ears, and on the head, armpits and thighs. Not only are ticks harmful by themselves, they will also lead to other infections if they are not removed. You can use tweezers to remove ticks, but be very careful if a tick is embedded in the skin. Always wear gloves while removing ticks.

When you remove a tick make sure that you dispose of it well

Bugs and Bites

There are other bugs that bother dogs and puppies. Flies are a major nuisance for your pet. Some flies can bite the ears and neck of your dog or puppy and leave red marks. Apply an antiseptic cream to the infected area if you find these marks. Also ensure that your pet does not go out during the hottest part of the day. Dogs and puppies can also come into contact with other insects, like wasps.

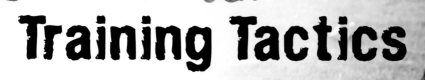
Training Tactics

You must teach your pet some basic manners and to be well behaved so that it is a pleasure to have at home.

The Initial Scare

When you first bring your dog or puppy home, it may be very submissive and scared. Your pet still won't recognize you well and may feel threatened by you or some other member of the family. Over a period of time, it will get over this initial scare and develop its own signals to indicate what it wants. It will also develop a relationship with every person in the home.

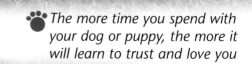
The more time you spend with your dog or puppy, the more it will learn to trust and love you

Higher Education

After your pet has got over the initial scare, you can teach it to follow basic instructions, like when and where to sit or eat. This teaching process may seem difficult, but it should be practiced by everyone at home. It is important to reward your pet when it has followed an instruction successfully. Getting a reward in the form of a biscuit or other treat will make it feel important and happy.

You need to be gentle with your dog or puppy while teaching it new tricks

22

By taking your dog or puppy for family outings you will make it feel welcome and a part of your family

Common Questions

What should I do if my dog or puppy bites me?

Initially your dog or puppy will not know whether it should bite or not. Do not allow it to place its mouth on your hand. Also do not put your face too close to your dog or puppy's face. If your pet does bite you, let your parents know immediately. They will help you deal with your dog or puppy.

Gentle Love

It is very important for you to be gentle with your pet. You can accompany an elder when your dog or puppy is being taken out for a walk or a visit to the vet. Never harm the animal by pulling its tail or dragging it by its collar or legs. Never hit your pet, no matter how angry you are.

Finding a Trainer

Even after you have trained your pet at home, you can consult a professional trainer to fine-tune its education.

Good Idea

Your new pet is like a small child. Whether you train it or not, it picks up the habits it sees around it. Professional training can help develop good habits and make it easier for you to bond with your pet. A dog or puppy that has received professional training usually becomes more obedient and responds well to instructions.

You should be gentle but firm when instructing your dog or puppy

Classes for Both

Usually, dogs and puppies are best trained in a group. Your pet will learn to interact with other dogs and to recognize you in a group of people. You can also pick up some handy tips when you watch other people interacting with their dogs or puppies. You can watch the training tactics used by the professionals and employ the same tactics at home.

An adult will help you find a trainer for your dog or puppy

!

Top Tips

Dogs are best trained when they are puppies. Puppies should start their professional training sessions when they are about two to three months old. During puppy training it is important to remember that they do not have the endurance of dogs. They are active for short amounts of time and need enough rest and sleep.

Which Trainer?

Looking for a good professional trainer is obviously the first step. Ask other dog owners for recommendations. Before making a decision, speak to people whose dogs have been with this trainer. Watch the trainer with other pets and observe if they have the mix of discipline and affection that will be best for your pet.

Your dog or puppy will learn to interact better when trained in a group with other dogs and puppies

Keeping Fit

It is important for your dog or puppy to get enough exercise and play so that it does not become sluggish or lazy.

Fat or Fit

Obesity in your dog or puppy is quite a seroius problem if not checked immediately. Dogs or puppies that are overweight are more prone to injury. Many tend to lose the sheen on their coats and develop dry skin. You could prevent it by making your pet excercise. You could also give diet food to your pet, but consult your vet first.

Give your dog or puppy enough exercise so that it does not become obese or face other health problems

Your dog or puppy initially might be scared of water but will follow you if you teach it to swim

Buy a leash and collar that is comfortable for your dog or puppy. Open the leash now and then to give it a sense of freedom

The Best Exercise

Exercise not only improves the health of your dog or puppy but also gives it the freedom to move about in a natural manner. An exercised dog or puppy rests more calmly at home and is also less nervous when left alone. Walking is good for all dogs or puppies. Remember to use a leash and a collar when you take your dog or puppy out for a walk. You do not have to run a marathon, just enjoyable light runs are enough! Make the walks interesting for your pet by carrying a toy with you. Allow it to play with other dogs. Most dogs love to chase and retrieve. Show your dog or puppy the toy, then throw it and encourage your pet to return it to you.

Common Questions

Do dogs or puppies swim?

Most dogs and puppies love to swim. Puppies especially might be scared of the water at first, but their confidence will grow with time. Introduce them to the water slowly if they are nervous.
Always make sure your pet has an easy way out of any body of water they are entering.

Summer Care

While summer may be great fun for you and your friends,
it may not be the same for your dog or puppy.

Too Hot to Handle

Have you seen your dog or puppy panting on a hot
summer day or after a run? This is how it cools
itself down. Since dogs do not sweat, it is difficult
to understand if your pet is feeling hot. During
summer you must check your pet regularly for
symptoms of heat stroke. These symptoms include
dry skin with very high temperature, rapid
heartbeat, vomiting and even collapsing. You
should cool your pet with cool water or spray it
with a hose (but be careful of its eyes and ears). If
you see any of these symptoms you should take
your dog or puppy to the vet as soon as possible.

*Your dog or puppy will
enjoy a nice cold shower
after playing on a hot
summer day*

Keep it Short

Dogs and puppies that spend a lot of time outdoors during hot summers are at risk from severe heat exhaustion. Do not play outdoors with your pet for a long time in summer. Give it cold water to drink, or let it lick ice cubes. This will help to bring down the body temperature and make your pet feel better.

Top Tips

The risk of fleas and ticks increases during the summer months, as does the bother from flies and other bugs. So check your pet more often and consult your vet if it needs medication.

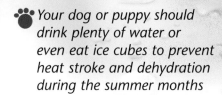
🐾 *Your dog or puppy should drink plenty of water or even eat ice cubes to prevent heat stroke and dehydration during the summer months*

Keep it Cool

Never leave your pet in a locked vehicle for long, especially in summer. The temperature inside the vehicle can rise rapidly, and your pet can overheat. If your dog or puppy has long hair and a heavy coat, giving it a haircut can make it feel less hot and more comfortable.

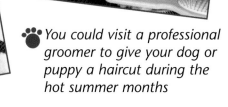
🐾 *You could visit a professional groomer to give your dog or puppy a haircut during the hot summer months*

Keeping Warm

Extreme cold can be harmful to your dog or puppy. So you must ensure that they are warm and snug.

A Snug Home

In winter, you should never leave your dog or puppy locked outdoors without proper shelter. If your pet's home is outside the house, make sure that it is raised from the ground and the floor is covered with dry straw or hay and not just a blanket, as blankets become damp in the cold weather. You should also cover the door of your pet's home with heavy plastic sheets to keep the chill out.

Don't let your dog or puppy sleep on the floor during the cold winter months

Wrapped Up

Make sure your pet does not contract hypothermia, which is a state when the body temperature drops to a level lower than normal. Check if your dog or puppy is shivering. This is the main symptom of hypothermia. As well as serious loss of body heat, the condition can also lead to a fluctuation in blood pressure and heart rate that can be fatal for your pet. If such a situation arises, wrap your dog or puppy in a warm blanket, make it drink a warm liquid and take it to the vet at once.

You could buy your dog or puppy a colorful and warm coat to keep them snug and stylish during winter

Biting Cold

Your pet may be affected by frostbite in winter — especially around its ears, toes and the tip of the tail. If you see any reddening or blistering in these areas, apply a warm (but not hot) pad to the affected area. Take your dog or puppy to the vet as soon as possible.

Look after your dog or puppy during winter to avoid frostbite

Common Questions

What should I do if the water in my pet's water bowl freezes over?

Use deep plastic bowls so that the water does not freeze quickly. Add warm water from time to time. If possible, move the water bowl to a warmer place, but make sure your dog or puppy has easy access to it at all times.

Happy Family

Your dog or puppy should fit into your home and be comfortable with all members of the family and any other pet that you may have.

Taking Care

Most dogs and puppies react in a very friendly and protective way when they see a new baby in the house. But you have to take some precautions to keep both the baby and the pet safe. Train it to be calm around the new baby. Do not allow your pet to play around the baby's crib. Your pet should be kept out of the baby's room. When a new baby joins the family it is more important than ever that the dog or puppy is kept in good health. Make sure that you de-flea them regularly and keep them up to date at the vets.

Never leave your dog or puppy alone with babies and young children

Living Together

Your dog or puppy can live peacefully with another pet in the house if trained to do so. In the beginning you must watch and supervise them when they are together. Remember that both dogs and cats are predators by nature and might not naturally get along. Slowly introduce your dog or puppy to your other pets and they should get used to each other.

It is important to know what breeds of dogs and puppies live well with other pets.

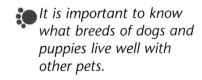

Sleeping Separately

Dogs and cats should have separate places to sleep. They should be fed separately and at different times. But most importantly, you will have to give each pet enough attention so that none feels neglected because of another.

!

Top Tips

When you bring your new dog or puppy home, stroke it and existing pets separately, but without washing your hands in between, so that their scents are exchanged. This is a good way for them get used to each other.

🐾 *In some cases you may have to use a cage or a pen to protect smaller pets*

While I'm Away

When you travel you have to decide whether you want to take your pet along or leave it behind.

On Vacation

If you decide to travel with your pet, you will have to spend some extra time planning your vacation and carry with you all the things that your pet may need. You also have to check all travel regulations and make sure that the plane or train and hotels allow your pet to be with you.

You could leave your dog or puppy with a friend or relative

Make sure that your dog or puppy has plenty to play with and gets lots of exercise while you are away

With Friends

You might leave your dog or puppy with a friend, neighbor or relative when you are away. It is a good idea to let the person take your dog or puppy a few days before you leave. Then you can occasionally help out while your pet gets used to its new surroundings. You could leave your dog or puppy at a kennel — but first ask your vet to recommend a good one.

Things to Remember

You should check out the dog kennel yourself. The basics that a kennel should provide includes:

- Clean space for indoor and outdoor exercise and play
- Daily walk service
- Good ventilation
- Clean bedding
- A variety of healthy and nutritious meals
- Necessary medicines
- A vaccination check
- Separate housing for old and infirm dogs

 *You should always visit a boarding kennel before you plan to leave your dog or puppy there when you are away on vacation*

Common Questions

Can my dog or puppy travel by air?

Check if the airline allows pets in the cabin — otherwise, you will have to place your pet in a carrier, which will go into the cargo hold. Always remember to put an identity tag on your pet.

Made For Each Other

A dog is a very loyal animal. Your dog or puppy can help you and your family in various ways.

A Friend in Need

Most breeds of dogs can be trained to become assistance dogs, also called guide dogs. They help and protect people with disabilities. They can help someone who cannot see to cross busy streets, use public transport and even find the way back home. Dogs can also be trained to recognize the sound of doorbells, phones, alarms or even the cry of a baby. Then they alert the person who cannot hear. But dogs need professional training to become assistance dogs, search dogs or police dogs.

Searching High and Low

Search dogs are used by the police to sniff for dangerous materials and by the fire service to find people trapped inside collapsed buildings or mines, or buried under snow. They are specially trained to carry first aid to the trapped person and to stay with them, if necessary, until help arrives. Shepherds have also used dogs for centuries to round up sheep.

Search dogs are considered to be the most highly trained canines in the world

BRIGADA CANINA

Top Tips

Some dogs are specially trained to help in the recovery of patients. These dogs are kept by hospitals and help to cheer up a person during the period of recovery. If the patient has a dog at home, it can also be trained to help the patient recover.

Sniffing Things

Some dogs are trained to sniff out drugs, explosives and even criminals! These dogs are trained to recognize a particular scent over time and then their sensitive noses are used to seek it out in the real world. They are used by police and security agencies all around the world to tackle crime.

German Shepherds make good watch dogs as well as sniffer dogs

Household Dangers

There are many things in your house that can cause harm to your dog or puppy. You have to take precautions and guard your pet against these dangers.

Poison

Poison for rats and cockroaches, as well as insecticides, should be kept out of reach of pets. If they mistake it for food and eat it, they can be very ill, or can even die. It is also advisable to keep medicines out of their reach. Also remember to not give any chocolate to your pet. In large quantities, chocolate can poison it!

Always label jars in the house as a safety measure

In The Garden

Plants in your garden must be selected carefully. They should not contain any substance that may cause your dog or puppy harm. You must make sure that there is no chemical fertilizer or pesticide in the garden that is within reach of your pet. If your pet consumes any of it then take it to the vet immediately.

Fertilizers or pesticides are potentially very dangerous to your dog or puppy

Choking Hazard

All dogs love bones, but you have to make sure your pet does not get any cooked or old bones, as they can crack into small splinters and choke the dog or puppy. For the same reason, never give your pet the bone of a chicken or any other bird. When you buy chewy toys for your pet, make sure these toys do not have removable small parts. These parts can choke a dog or puppy if swallowed.

Common Questions

Is antifreeze dangerous to pets?

Antifreeze contains a sweet chemical called ethylene glycol. This can attract animals. But antifreeze is very poisonous so keep it out of reach.

Treat your dog or puppy like a small child and always give it things that can be chewed easily without causing any harm

Vet and Vaccination

It is important to have a vet who is familiar with your dog or puppy. You should take your pet for regular medical check-ups and vaccinations.

Selecting a Vet

Ask any friends or relatives who have a dog or puppy to recommend a good vet. Then, before you bring your pet home, visit the vet and satisfy yourself that they and their team are suitable to treat your dog or puppy. Your vetinarian should be open to you looking around and asking any questions you have, but be careful not to interupt their work. Once you have bought your dog or puppy, book an initial consultation with your vet as soon as possible.

The Adviser

Even when your pet is perfectly healthy, the vet is your adviser about a number of things, like the kind of food you should give, the kind of housing needed, the training of your pet and where to leave your pet if you are going on a vacation. So stay in touch with your vet.

A regular visit to the vet is an important part of caring for your pet.

Vaccines

It is important to get your dog or puppy vaccinated as soon as you bring it home. A proper vaccination program protects your pet and everyone else at home. The program will vary from breed to breed and your vet will explain exactly what your dog or puppy needs. The dog or puppy may initially react to a vaccine. It may sleep for many hours at a stretch or lose its appetite for some time. Ask your vet about possible reactions, so that you are not scared without reason.

Follow your vet's vaccination schedule closely. This will help your pet become familiar with the vet and will keep them healthy

Top Tips

Some dogs or puppies may react to vaccines more strongly than others. Do alert your vet if this happens to your pet, but this is no reason to stop the vaccination program.

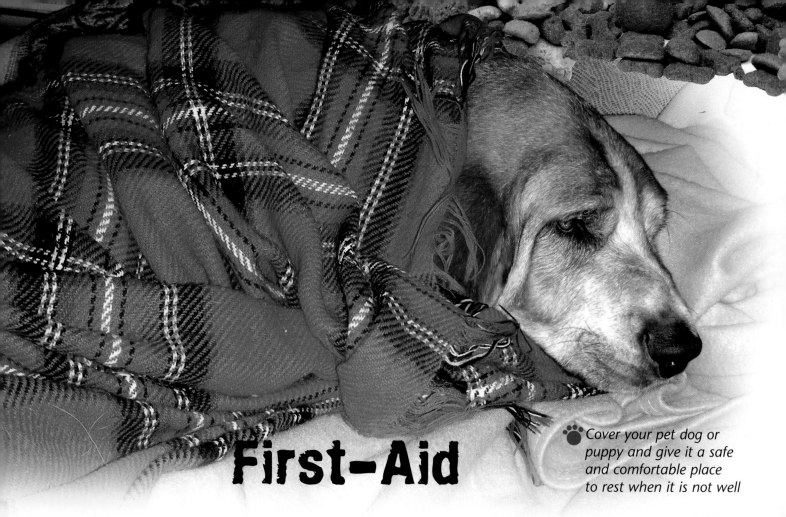

First-Aid

Cover your pet dog or puppy and give it a safe and comfortable place to rest when it is not well

If your dog has a minor injury or a mild illness, you should be able to handle the situation at home.

Ill at Home

Many of the illnesses that we suffer from can affect dogs and puppies too. The difference is that they cannot tell us what is wrong with them - but they will convey it through some signs. Your pet becomes less active when it is not well. If it is a mild illness which the pet had earlier and for which the vet had already prescribed a medicine, check with an adult that they have been given their medicine correctly. Never give your pet any medicine that has not been prescribed by the vet.

Allergic

Many dogs and puppies are allergic to fleas, pollen, dust mites in the carpet and some varieties of dog food as well. An allergic reaction can make your pet scratch itself, making the skin sore. These allergies can also lead to digestive problems. If you suspect your dog or puppy is suffering from an allergic reaction to something, consult your vet.

Your pet may become irritable when it is sick. Make sure it has somewhere comfortable and quiet to rest

First-Aid Kit

You should keep a first-aid kit at home. Common items for the first-aid kit are gauze and elastic bandages, band-aids, cotton balls, antibiotic ointment, eyewash, vaseline, bandage scissors, blanket, tweezers, muzzle and thermometer.

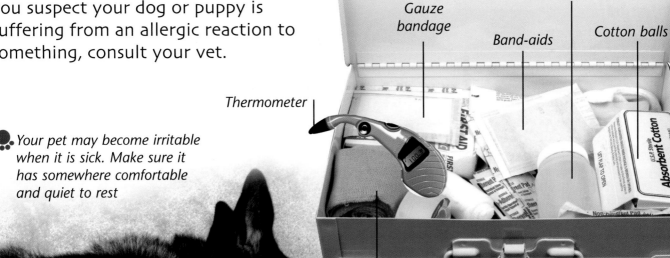

Antiseptic lotion

Gauze bandage

Band-aids

Cotton balls

Thermometer

Elastic bandage

Always keep a first aid kit handy at home to deal with small emergencies

Common Question

Can I tell if my dog or puppy is ill by looking at its coat?

In some cases, yes you can. Sometimes, when your pet falls ill, its coat will lose its shine and maybe some hair. This is sometimes the first indication of illness in a dog or puppy.

Glossary

Choking: Causing suffocation

Communicate: To convey one's feeling

Dehydration: Lack of water

Distracted: Having your attention diverted

Endurance: Ability to bear hardship

Exhaustion: Tiredness

Fleas: Small insects that suck blood from animals

Frostbite: Damage to the body due to extreme cold

Grooming: Cleaning

Hyperactivity: Excessive activity

Irritable: Easily annoyed

Kennel: House for a dog

Predators: Animals that hunt other animals

Recommendations: Advice

Regulations: Rules

Responsibility: Taking care

Temperament: Character

Ticks: Blood sucking insects that are a little larger than fleas

Tweezers: Pluckers

Vaccines: Injections to prevent diseases

Vet: A doctor who treats animals

Index